Inside the NFL

THE
KANSAS CITY
CHIEFS

BOB ITALIA
ABDO & Daughters

1

Published by Abdo & Daughters, 4940 Viking Drive, Suite 622, Edina, Minnesota 55435.

Copyright © 1996 by Abdo Consulting Group, Inc., Pentagon Tower, P.O. Box 36036, Minneapolis, Minnesota 55435 USA. International copyrights reserved in all countries. No part of this book may be reproduced in any form without written permission from the publisher.

Printed in the United States.

Cover Photo credits: Wide World Photos/Allsport
Interior Photo credits: Allsport, page 22
                         Wide World Photos, pages 4, 5, 7, 9, 12, 15, 17-19,
                                            21, 23, 24, 27, 28
                         Bettmann Photos, pages 6, 10, 13, 27

Edited by Kal Gronvall

Library of Congress Cataloging-in-Publication Data

Italia, Bob, 1955—
        The Kansas City Chiefs / Bob Italia
                p.   cm. — (Inside the NFL)
        Includes index.
        Summary: Describes the formation, history, and key personalities
        of the AFL team that won its first and only Super bowl in 1969.
        ISBN 1-56239-533-5
        1. Kansas City Chiefs (football team)—juvenile literature. [1. Kansas
        City Chiefs (football team) 2. football—history.]
        I. Title. II. Series: Italia, Bob, 1955— Inside the NFL.
        GV956.K35I83   1996
        796.332'64'0978139—dc20
                                                              95-25471
                                                              CIP
                                                              AC

CONTENTS

Glory Days

In 1969, the Kansas City Chiefs won their first and only Super Bowl with a team made of their biggest stars. There was quarterback Len Dawson, wide receiver Otis Taylor, running back Mike Garrett, and middle linebacker Willie Lanier.

Since those glory days, the Chiefs remained relatively quiet, having endured the longest playoff drought in team history. Defensive end Neil Smith and linebacker Derrick Thomas emerged as defensive stars who often carried the team. But not even the addition of quarterback Joe Montana could boost the Chiefs to the Super Bowl. For that to happen, the Chiefs need to fill the holes in their defense while the search goes on for a top-notch quarterback.

Kansas City Chiefs coach Hank Stram is carried off the field after the Chiefs won Super Bowl IV.

Otis Taylor, wide receiver for the Kansas City Chiefs.

The Dallas Texans

The Kansas City Chiefs were originally the Dallas Texans, one of the first teams of the American Football League (AFL), which formed in 1960.

Owner Lamar Hunt wanted his team to play in his home state. But the NFL also had a football team in Dallas—the Cowboys. The Texans were not popular with Dallas football fans. The Cowboys drew bigger crowds even though they had losing records in 1960 and 1961.

The Dallas Texans were losing money. Hunt could either fold or move his team. Since the Texans were important to Hunt, he decided to find another city where his team could play.

Dallas Texans'
Dave Webster (21)
defends against
New York Titans'
Art Powell.

Len Dawson
and Company

While Hunt shopped for another city, coach Hank Stram prepared for the 1962 season. He had signed quarterback Len Dawson, who had five years of NFL experience, playing for the Pittsburgh Steelers and the Cleveland Browns. Dawson had much potential, but was inconsistent.

Stram worked with Dawson and improved his practicing habits. The work paid off as the Texans rolled to an 11-3 record and won the AFL Western Division. Halfback Abner Haynes scored 21 touchdowns and set a league record. Fullback Curtis McClinton was named AFL Rookie of the Year. The defense, led by linemen Buck Buchanan and Jerry Mays, and linebackers E.J. Holub and Bobby Bell, was one of the league's best.

In the 1962 league championship game, Dallas beat the Houston Oilers 20-17 in sudden-death overtime. Dawson was named AFL Player of the Year.

Despite the success, the Texans had poor attendance. After the season, the Texans moved to Kansas City and became the Chiefs.

Kansas City quarterback Len Dawson.

Goin' to Kansas City

The change of scenery changed the team's fortunes. In 1963, Kansas City finished third in the Western Division with a 5-7-2 record. The next season, the Chiefs improved to 7-7. But no one knew why the team could not return to championship form. One area Stram wanted to improve was his receiving corps. Though Dawson threw 30 touchdown passes, the Chiefs' wide receivers were considered slow.

In 1965, the Chiefs drafted Otis Taylor. The six-foot, three-inch, 215-pound Taylor was a huge wide receiver with blinding speed. His impact was immediate as the Chiefs finished 7-5-2. But the team could not overcome the tragic death of fullback Mack Lee Hill, who died during midseason knee surgery, or the loss of Abner Haynes, who was traded.

Still, the Chiefs seemed on the verge of greatness again, with strong defensive players like Jerry Mays, Buck Buchanan, E.J. Holub, Sherrill Headrick, Bobby Bell, Fred Williamson, and Johnny Robinson. If the offense came around, the Chiefs would be hard to beat. The following season, few teams challenged them.

Otis Taylor makes a one-handed catch against the Buffalo Bills in 1971.

Super Bowl I

In 1966, the Chiefs signed Mike Garrett. He gave the Chiefs a dangerous breakaway runner who sparked the offense. The Chiefs swept through the season with an impressive 11-2-1 record and won the Western Division. Then they defeated the Buffalo Bills in the league championship game. But there was one more foe to conquer.

In 1966, the AFL champion Chiefs played the NFL champion Green Bay Packers in the first-ever AFL-NFL Championship Game. Hunt thought the name of the championship game was too long and clumsy.

"Why don't we just call it the Super Bowl?" Hunt said. The name has stuck ever since.

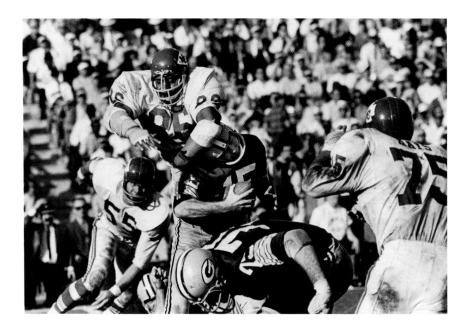

The Chiefs defense smothers Green Bay quarterback Bart Starr in Super Bowl I.

The Chiefs were big underdogs against the powerful Packers. Many experts considered the AFL as a minor-league organization. But more than 65 million people watched the televised game—the largest single audience for an athletic event in the history of television.

The Chiefs matched Green Bay's early score with Dawson's 7-yard pass to fullback Curtis McClinton. Kansas City trailed 14-10 at halftime, but then fell apart in the second half. Behind quarterback Bart Starr, the Packers cruised to a 35-10 victory as Green Bay stopped Taylor and Garrett while pressuring Dawson on every pass play.

The 1967 season was a big letdown. The pass defense faltered, and by the time adjustments were made, the Chiefs finished 9-5-0. The play of rookies Willie Lanier and placekicker Jan Stenerud were the season's highlights.

Kansas City rebounded in 1968, finishing 12-2. But so did the Oakland Raiders, who beat the Chiefs 41-6 in the playoff game for first place. Injuries to Taylor, Garrett, and McClinton hurt their postseason plans. Rookie fullback Robert Holmes was the biggest surprise. The 14th-round draft pick finished with 866 rushing yards, and set the stage for next year's incredible season.

A Super Return

In 1969, the Chiefs finished second in the Western Division, but then won playoff games over the New York Jets and the Oakland Raiders. With the postseason wins, Kansas City became the first AFL team to play in two Super Bowls.

Their opponent was the Minnesota Vikings, who were 13-point favorites. The Vikings had a great defense led by "The Purple People Eaters," a defensive line known for its ferocious pass rush. The Chiefs weren't impressed. They felt their defense was great, too. They also felt their offense could handle any pass rush they faced.

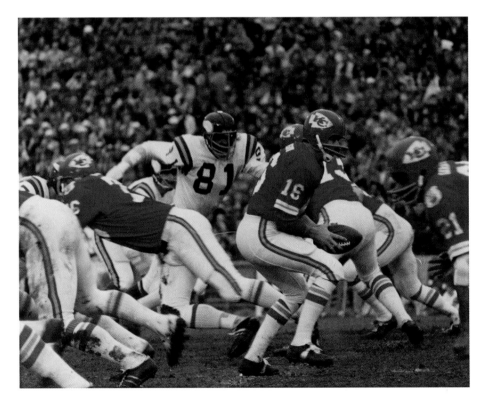

Minnesota Vikings Carl Eller rushes Len Dawson in Super Bowl IV.

In the first half, Kansas City dominated Minnesota. Dawson led the Chiefs on three long drives, but they had to settle for three Jan Stenerud field goals. The Kansas City defensive linemen, meanwhile, put constant pressure on Vikings quarterback Joe Kapp, forcing him to hurry his passes.

Late in the second quarter, Dawson drove Kansas City to the Vikings 5-yard line. On third down, Minnesota expected a pass. As Dawson rolled to his right, the Vikings chased him. But then Dawson handed the ball to Mike Garrett who ran left and into the end zone. The Vikings were stunned as they fell behind 16-0.

Minnesota linebacker Roy Winston climbs over Robert Holmes as he rushes Len Dawson.

The Vikings rallied for a touchdown early in the third quarter and appeared to have the momentum. But the Chiefs began another scoring drive. On the Vikings 46-yard line, Dawson faded back and threw a short, sideline pass to Taylor. Taylor broke two tackles and ran for a touchdown, giving the Chiefs a 23-7 lead. The Chiefs held the Vikings scoreless the rest of the way.

Dawson was named the game's Most Valuable Player. He played almost flawlessly, completing 12 of 17 passes. Not only did the Chiefs score a huge victory for the AFL, Kansas City had the makings of a football dynasty. Only time would tell.

The Longest Game

The NFL and AFL merged in 1970. The Chiefs found themselves in the American Football Conference's powerful Western Division with the Oakland Raiders, Denver Broncos, and San Diego Chargers—teams that would dominate the AFC for many years.

Oakland won the AFC West in 1970. Kansas City won the division title in 1971. In the first round of the playoffs, the Chiefs hosted the Miami Dolphins on Christmas Day.

The Chiefs and Dolphins played seesaw all day. Finally, Dawson hit Elmo Wright on a 63-yard touchdown pass to give the Chiefs a 24-17 fourth-quarter lead. But Miami would not give in. They tied the score with 90 seconds remaining. Still, there was time for one more score. Dawson drove Kansas City into field-goal range, but Stenerud missed the kick. The game went into sudden-death overtime.

Both Stenerud and Dolphins kicker Garo Yepremian had field goal chances, but both missed. The game went into a second overtime— only the second time in pro football history. Yepremian got another chance midway through the overtime period. This time, his field goal split the uprights, and the Dolphins won 27-24. The longest game in NFL history was finally over. The Chiefs and Dolphins had battled 82 minutes and 40 seconds. It was the last game played in Kansas City's Municipal Stadium.

Joe Delaney

In 1972, the Chiefs moved to the new 80,000-seat Arrowhead Stadium. The Chiefs kept winning in 1972 and 1973, but they didn't make the playoffs. After a 5-9 season in 1974, Stram was fired. A year later, Dawson and Taylor retired. Only Willie Lanier remained from the glory days, and he was hardly enough. The Chiefs slid to the bottom of the AFC West in the late 1970s and stayed there.

The Chiefs had quarterback and running back problems. MacArthur Lane, Tony Reed, and Ted McKnight did their best, but were not consistent.

The Chiefs struggled until 1980, when new coach Marv Levy led Kansas City to an 8-8 record. But Levy expected bigger things in 1981 because of rookie running back Joe Delaney.

Delaney came from Northwestern State University in Louisiana. He was small but fast. In his rookie year, Delaney gained 1,121 yards—a Kansas City team record. For his efforts, Delaney was named AFC Rookie of the Year.

Joe Delaney leaps over Buccaneers defenders.

The 9-7 Chiefs nearly made the playoffs in 1981, but injuries and inconsistent quarterback play hurt their playoff chances. The 1982 players' strike wiped out almost half the season. Still, Delaney had another great season. Already, Delaney was considered one of the best backs in the game.

On June 29, 1983, in Monroe, Louisiana, tragedy struck. Delaney was on a lakeshore playing catch with some friends when he heard cries for help. Three boys were drowning in the lake. Delaney wasn't much of a swimmer. But he jumped in the water to try to save the boys. One reached the shore. Two drowned. The 24-year-old Delaney didn't make it either. With Delaney gone, the Chiefs fell to last place in 1983. Levy was fired. John Mackovic replaced him.

Mackovic built a winning team around quarterback Bill Kenney and an excellent defensive secondary that featured safeties Deron Cherry and Lloyd Burruss and cornerbacks Albert Lewis and Kevin Ross. On offense, Kenney often passed to Henry Marshall, J.T. Smith, Carlos Carson, and Stephone Paige.

In 1986, the Chiefs made the playoffs but lost in the first round to the New York Jets. Despite the success, Mackovic was fired because of problems with the players. Frank Ganz replaced Mackovic, but the Chiefs did not play well.

The Nigerian Nightmare

In 1987, Kansas City drafted six-foot three-inch, 260-pound running back Christian Okoye. Okoye grew up in Nigeria. He came to the United States on a track scholarship to Azusa Pacific University in California. While at Azusa, Okoye took an interest in football. So he asked the track coach if he could play for Azusa's football team. A few years later, he joined the team.

Okoye wasn't used much during Ganz's two years with the Chiefs. But in 1989, new coach Marty Schottenheimer decided to give Okoye the ball. As a result, Okoye led the NFL in rushing.

The defense, led by AFC Defensive Rookie of the Year Derrick Thomas, became one of the NFL's best. The defensive backfield had Deron Cherry,

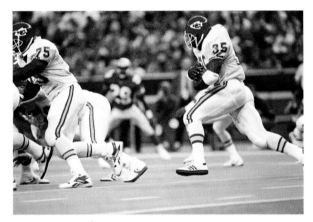

Running back Christian Okoye.

Lloyd Burruss, and Albert Lewis. Linebacker Dino Hackett and nose tackle Bill Maas were tough against the run.

Despite Okoye's rushing, the Chiefs still needed a passing attack. Quarterback Steve DeBerg started in 1989, but Steve Pelluer challenged him. Having spent his first NFL years with the Dallas Cowboys, Pelluer showed potential. But he needed more consistency.

Wide receiver Otis Taylor joins the Chiefs in 1965.

*Kansas
Ch*

Quarterback Len Dawson is named M.V.P. in Super Bowl IV.

Coach Hank Stram leads Kansas City to a Super Bowl win in 1969.

*Kansas City
Chiefs*

40　　　　　　　20　　　　10

Running back Joe Delaney is named AFC Rookie of the Year in 1981.

s City

efs

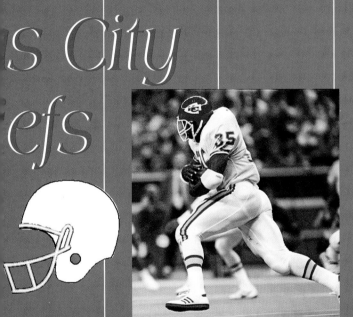

Quarterback Joe Montana joins the Chiefs in 1993.

Running back Christian Okoye leads the NFL in rushing in 1989.

40　　　　30　　　　20　　　　10

Kansas City Chiefs

A Playoff Return

Coach Schottenheimer was used to winning. He led the Cleveland Browns to three straight AFC Central Division titles before joining Kansas City. With Okoye and a strong defense, the Chiefs were ready to recapture their winning tradition. Kansas City fans had not seen a home playoff game since the memorable double-overtime loss to Miami in 1971.

In 1990, Schottenheimer got the Chiefs into the playoffs with an 11-5 record. Much of the success was due to an opportunistic defense that accounted for 60 sacks, 6 blocked punts, 25 fumble recoveries and 20 pass interceptions. Derrick Thomas led the way with 20 sacks, and safety Deron Cherry made a strong comeback from injury.

Quarterback Steve DeBerg had a great year despite playing the last few games with a broken finger on his passing hand. He connected for 23 touchdowns and only 4 interceptions. Okoye was bothered by injuries much of the season. But Barry Word racked up impressive yardage.

In the playoffs, the Chiefs faced the Dolphins in Miami. Kansas City jumped out to a 10-3 halftime lead and tacked on two Lowry field goals in the third quarter for a 16-3 advantage. But Miami stormed back in the fourth quarter with two Dan Marino touchdown passes as they took the game 17-16. It was a disappointing loss. But the Chiefs had a strong young team that would only get better.

In 1991, the Chiefs experienced an up-and-down season. The offense showed an inability to make the big plays, so the Chiefs relied on their ground game. The combination of Okoye and Word piled up 1,715 yards rushing and 13 touchdowns. But rookie Harvey Williams drew the praise in limited action. The defense remained strong, with end Neil Smith and linebacker Derrick Thomas starring in front of an average secondary. The Chiefs finished with a 10-6 record and made the playoffs for the second straight year.

This time, in the first round, Kansas City stayed home to play the L.A. Raiders. It was a tough, defensive struggle as the Chiefs seized a slim 7-3 halftime lead. The Raiders drew within 7-6 after the third quarter, and visions of last year's fourth-quarter playoff collapse filled the stadium. But the defense held firm as the Chiefs added a field goal for a 10-6 victory. The win gave them the right to travel to Buffalo to play the AFC-champion Bills on January 6. The outcome was predictable, with the Bills coasting to an easy 37-14 win.

Coach Marty Shottenheimer.

The Quarterback Shuffle

Despite the playoff loss, the Chiefs were making great strides. Management knew their current team was good enough to get to the Super Bowl. If only they had a top-notch quarterback. So in 1992, they signed a proven winner—quarterback Dave Krieg. The missing piece of the puzzle seemed to be in place. Now the Chiefs had to prove they were Super Bowl contenders.

The season did not progress as the team had expected. The Chiefs needed three defensive touchdowns in their last game to even make the playoffs. An 8-4 start evaporated into a struggle for the playoffs as the Chiefs finished 10-6. Even though they qualified for postseason play for the third straight year, the season was a disappointment. The offense was inconsistent, and Word, Okoye, and Williams totaled only 1,317 yards amongst them. Neil Smith and Derrick Thomas each had 14.5 sacks, and were the season's bright spot. In the first round of the playoffs, Kansas City traveled to San Diego. There, they were shutout 17-0.

Management was frustrated. The Chiefs seemed to be stuck. They needed solid play from their quarterback spot. But none of the current players could get the job done. So Kansas City went all out and signed legendary quarterback Joe Montana.

Derrick Thomas had 14.5 quarterback sacks in 1992.

Joe Montana

Montana had just finished a disappointing season with the San Francisco 49ers in which he spent most of the year on the bench after elbow surgery. He felt it was time for a change. The Chiefs were happy to oblige him. Joining him was longtime veteran running back Marcus Allen. Both proved to be the biggest surprises of the 1993 season.

The 11-5 Chiefs advanced to the AFC championship game that season, further than at any time since 1969, when they won their only Super Bowl. After finishing 25th in offense in 1992, the Chiefs made big changes, including new offensive coordinator Paul Hackett. Because of injuries, Montana missed five games and played in only 38 of 64 quarters. But he was the AFC's second-ranked passer.

Allen was the NFL's Comeback Player of the Year as he rushed for 764 yards and tied for a league-high 15 touchdowns. On the other side of the ball, defensive end Neil Smith recorded an NFL-best 15 sacks. The Chiefs finally had a chance to win it all.

Joe Montana talks with former Chiefs quarterback Steve DeBerg.

Joe Montana quarterbacking the Chiefs.

In the first round, however, they locked into a duel with the Pittsburgh Steelers in Kansas City. Montana worked his old magic as he rallied his team with two fourth-quarter touchdowns for a 24-24 regulation tie. In overtime, Montana directed a drive that led to a Nick Lowry 32-yard, game-winning field goal. The Chiefs were on their way.

The second-round game against the Oilers in Houston was even more dramatic. Houston jumped out to a 10-0 halftime lead before the Chiefs struck for a third-quarter touchdown that made it 10-7. The Oilers tacked on a field goal for a 13-7 lead, but Montana threw two touchdown passes to vault the Chiefs into a 21-13 advantage. Houston rallied for a touchdown of their own that made it 21-20. But Marcus Allen sealed the win with an electrifying 21-yard touchdown run. The 28-20 win put the Chiefs into the AFC championship game in Buffalo against the Bills.

Most of the nation rooted for Montana to work his magic once again. But he completed only 9 of 23 passes for 125 yards. Even worse, he was knocked out of the game in the third quarter with a concussion, and backup Dave Krieg could only manage one touchdown for the Chiefs, who lost 30-13. Fans could only hope that Montana had enough left in him to make another Super Bowl run in 1994.

The Last Hurrah

Montana would rally the Chiefs. But it turned out to be his last hurrah. After beating the Indianapolis Colts 30-10 in Week 3, the Chiefs were 3-0 for the first time since 1966. In the win, Montana passed for 361 yards.

The following week, however, the L.A. Rams shocked the Chiefs 16-0 in Kansas City. It was the first shutout in Montana's 16-year career. He was intercepted three times. After a Week 6 loss to the San Diego Chargers, Montana worked his fourth-quarter magic against the Denver Broncos. Trailing 28-24 with 1:29 left in the game, Montana led Kansas City 75 yards in 9 plays, including the game-winning touchdown with 8 seconds remaining. It gave him 30 fourth-quarter comeback victories in his NFL career.

By Week 10, the Chiefs were 6-3 and trailed the first-place Chargers by one game. But a Week 11 loss to San Diego put them two games behind at 6-4. A crucial loss in Week 14 to Denver put the Chiefs at 7-6 and in danger of missing the playoffs. The slide continued until Week 16 when the Chiefs won 31-9 over Houston. But now they were 8-7 and in third place in the AFC West—two games behind San Diego and a game behind the L.A. Raiders. The season would all come down to the final game against the Raiders.

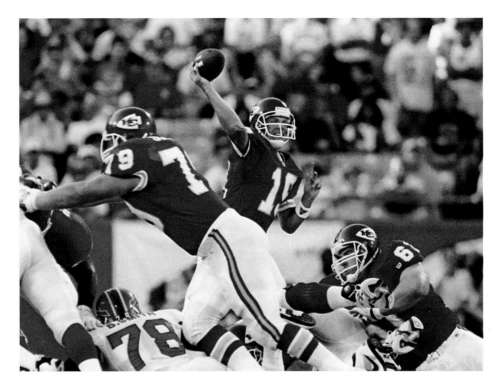

Joe Montana and the Chiefs against the Buffalo Bills.

It was the veterans who led the way. Montana threw a 47-yard touchdown pass to Willie Davis, and Marcus Allen rushed 33 times for 132 yards. Their 19-9 victory earned the Chiefs the final playoff spot and set up a match with Dan Marino and the Dolphins in Miami.

The two great quarterbacks got into a shoot-out, resulting in a 17-17 halftime score. But it was Marino, not Montana, who stayed hot in the second half as the Chiefs lost 27-17. In defeat, Montana passed for 314 yards. But it wasn't enough. Before the next season began, Montana announced his retirement.

The Key to Success

The Chiefs remained a talented team without Montana at the helm. But replacing him would not be an easy task. Even more, Kansas City was showing its age, and it remained to be seen whether the veterans like Thomas and Smith had enough in them to lead the Chiefs into the playoffs. As Montana had proved, the quarterback position would be the key to their success.

The Chiefs are relying on Neil Smith to lead them into the playoffs.

GLOSSARY

ALL-PRO—A player who is voted to the Pro Bowl.

BACKFIELD—Players whose position is behind the line of scrimmage.

CORNERBACK—Either of two defensive halfbacks stationed a short distance behind the linebackers and relatively near the sidelines.

DEFENSIVE END—A defensive player who plays on the end of the line and often next to the defensive tackle.

DEFENSIVE TACKLE—A defensive player who plays on the line and between the guard and end.

ELIGIBLE—A player who is qualified to be voted into the Hall of Fame.

END ZONE—The area on either end of a football field where players score touchdowns.

EXTRA POINT—The additional one-point score added after a player makes a touchdown. Teams earn extra points if the placekicker kicks the ball through the uprights of the goalpost, or if an offensive player crosses the goal line with the football before being tackled.

FIELD GOAL—A three-point score awarded when a placekicker kicks the ball through the uprights of the goalpost.

FULLBACK—An offensive player who often lines up farthest behind the front line.

FUMBLE—When a player loses control of the football.

GUARD—An offensive lineman who plays between the tackles and center.

GROUND GAME—The running game.

HALFBACK—An offensive player whose position is behind the line of scrimmage.

HALFTIME—The time period between the second and third quarters of a football game.

INTERCEPTION—When a defensive player catches a pass from an offensive player.

KICK RETURNER—An offensive player who returns kickoffs.

LINEBACKER—A defensive player whose position is behind the line of scrimmage.

LINEMAN—An offensive or defensive player who plays on the line of scrimmage.

PASS—To throw the ball.

PASS RECEIVER—An offensive player who runs pass routes and catches passes.

PLACEKICKER—An offensive player who kicks extra points and field goals. The placekicker also kicks the ball from a tee to the opponent after his team has scored.

PLAYOFFS—The postseason games played amongst the division winners and wild card teams which determines the Super Bowl champion.

PRO BOWL—The postseason All-Star game which showcases the NFL's best players.

PUNT—To kick the ball to the opponent.

QUARTER—One of four 15-minute time periods that makes up a football game.

QUARTERBACK—The backfield player who usually calls the signals for the plays.

REGULAR SEASON—The games played after the preseason and before the playoffs.

ROOKIE—A first-year player.

RUNNING BACK—A backfield player who usually runs with the ball.

RUSH—To run with the football.

SACK—To tackle the quarterback behind the line of scrimmage.

SAFETY—A defensive back who plays behind the linemen and linebackers. Also, two points awarded for tackling an offensive player in his own end zone when he's carrying the ball.

SPECIAL TEAMS—Squads of football players who perform special tasks (for example, kickoff team and punt-return team).

SPONSOR—A person or company that finances a football team.

SUPER BOWL—The NFL championship game played between the AFC champion and the NFC champion.

T FORMATION—An offensive formation in which the fullback lines up behind the center and quarterback with one halfback stationed on each side of the fullback.

TACKLE—An offensive or defensive lineman who plays between the ends and the guards.

TAILBACK—The offensive back farthest from the line of scrimmage.

TIGHT END—An offensive lineman who is stationed next to the tackles, and who usually blocks or catches passes.

TOUCHDOWN—When one team crosses the goal line of the other team's end zone. A touchdown is worth six points.

TURNOVER—To turn the ball over to an opponent either by a fumble, an interception, or on downs.

UNDERDOG—The team that is picked to lose the game.

WIDE RECEIVER—An offensive player who is stationed relatively close to the sidelines and who usually catches passes.

WILD CARD—A team that makes the playoffs without winning its division.

ZONE PASS DEFENSE—A pass defense method where defensive backs defend a certain area of the playing field rather than individual pass receivers.

INDEX